M

SOUTH AFRICA

ABDO
Publishing Company

SOUTH AFRICA

by Christie Rose Ritter

Content Consultant
Robert Edgar
Professor of African Studies, Howard University

CREDITS

Published by ABDO Publishing Company, 8000 West 78th Street, Edina, Minnesota 55439. Copyright © 2012 by Abdo Consulting Group, Inc. International copyrights reserved in all countries. No part of this book may be reproduced in any form without written permission from the publisher. The Essential Library™ is a trademark and logo of ABDO Publishing Company.

Printed in the United States of America,
North Mankato, Minnesota
062011
092011

Editor: Melissa York
Copy Editor: Susan M. Freese
Series design and cover production: Emily Love
Interior production: Kazuko Collins

About the Author: Christie Rose Ritter is an award-winning journalist who has written for newspapers, magazines, and websites. Her writing awards include First Place recognition in Environment/Agriculture, Features, and Science/Health from the Society of Professional Journalists.

Library of Congress Cataloging-in-Publication Data
Ritter, Christie R.
  South Africa / by Christie Rose Ritter.
     p. cm. -- (Countries of the world)
  Includes bibliographical references.
  ISBN 978-1-61783-118-8
  1. South Africa--Juvenile literature. 1. Title. II. Series: Countries of the world (Edina, Minn.)
  DT1719.R58 2012
  968--dc23
                          2011019251

Cover: Aerial view of Cape Town, South Africa

TABLE OF CONTENTS

CHAPTER 1

A VISIT TO SOUTH AFRICA

"Attention passengers: our next port of call will be Cape Town, South Africa!"

As you disembark on your cruise around the world, you are eager with anticipation. You've heard of Nelson Mandela, and you watched the 2010 World Cup in South Africa, but you know that there is much more to discover about this nation at the southernmost tip of Africa.

You disembark at the Victoria and Albert Waterfront in the city of Cape Town. The area was first developed when South Africa was a British colony, and it was recently revitalized as a new destination for tourists and locals alike as a place to shop, eat, and enjoy the harbor. You are eager to walk the streets of Cape Town—a modern, culturally vibrant, and diverse city.

View from the waterfront, Cape Town, South Africa

As you head away from the port and begin exploring the city, you browse through the stalls at leafy Greenmarket Square where vendors are selling unique artisan crafts. You look at woven baskets, colorful beaded necklaces, and pottery in all shapes and sizes. Strolling down the streets dotted with office towers and luxurious hotels, you are drawn toward the wonderful smells: curry, nutmeg, cardamom, and other exotic spices. Scents are also wafting toward you from restaurants serving the cuisines of India, Nigeria, Indonesia, and China.

Do you feel like a hike? You're in luck, because the iconic Table Mountain looms over Cape Town. It's a strenuous three-hour trek up the mountain, but the views are worth it. If you're running short on time or energy, you can take the aerial tramway to the top of the peak. From here, you can see the city spread out below you.

VICTORIA AND ALBERT WATERFRONT

The Victoria and Albert Waterfront—or the V&A, as locals call it—is a great place to grab a seat on a restaurant balcony and watch ships come and go. It has been a busy, working harbor for three centuries, but after a revitalization project in the 1990s, it has also become a fun place to visit. Today, the V&A is one of South Africa's top destinations. People come to hear local musicians and dancers, catch a movie, browse trendy shops, grab a bite to eat, and visit the aquarium.

Climbers can see Cape Town and the ocean
from the top of Table Mountain.

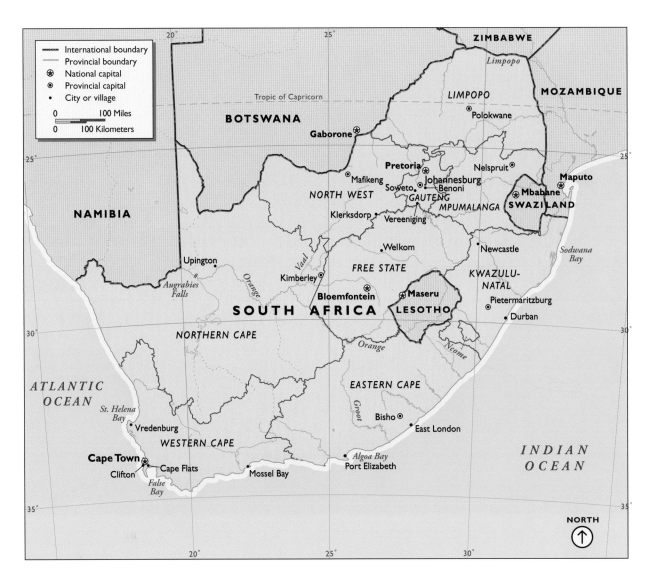

Political Boundaries of South Africa

In some ways, cosmopolitan Cape Town is just like any modern US or European city. But take a short drive out of the city, and wild Africa awaits your discovery. Along the rugged coast, near where the Indian and Atlantic Oceans meet, you will find yourself face to face with wild baboons. Watch out! They love to snatch shiny things, so hold on to your camera.

SOUTH AFRICA'S CONTRASTS

South Africa is a place of stark contrasts: modern and wild, rich and poor, black and white. The diverse neighborhoods of Cape Town tell the stories of the people who live there. Hugging the western slope of Table Mountain is the resort town of Clifton, with its white sandy beaches. Here, expensive homes and even swimming pools are built into the sides of the steep mountain.

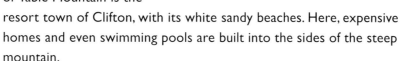

ANIMALS IN SOUTH AFRICA

To see lions and other native African wildlife requires a visit to an animal reserve. The Europeans who came to South Africa believed it was great sport to hunt some of Africa's most majestic animals. For example, lions were once widely distributed in the region, but their numbers were quickly reduced due to widespread hunting. Reserves were created to protect the animals and allow them to live in their native habitat. In one of South Africa's many reserves, it is possible to see what are referred to as Africa's "Big Five" animals: lions, leopards, elephants, Cape buffalo, and rhinoceroses.

CAPE FLATS

The majority of Cape Town's population lives in an area of townships, or settlements, called Cape Flats. Cape Flats is a sandy and marshy stretch of land east of Cape Town. This neighborhood was not anyone's first choice when selecting a place to build a home. But in the 1950s, the white-ruled government began forcing many South Africans to relocate here. The government wanted only whites to live in the central districts, close to schools and jobs. People of other races and ethnicities had to leave the city and build new homes out of whatever materials they could find. Residents of Cape Flats scavenged what materials they could: corrugated tin for roofs and plastic tarps for walls. People who had a little money or some good luck in scavenging used cement blocks or perhaps bricks to build slightly sturdier structures. It was not unusual for a dozen family members to live together in a two-room house. Until the 1980s, most homes had no electricity or running water.

Today, people in South Africa have the freedom to live where they want, but many are quite poor and cannot afford to buy or build homes elsewhere. The estimated population of the townships of Cape Flats is more than 2 million people.

But just a few miles to the southeast, millions of people live in a cluster of settlements called Cape Flats. Their lives are very different. Many of the people who live here struggle to provide food to feed their families, and many people suffer from serious health problems. Often, children have to leave school at an early age to help support their families.

DIVERSITY

Poverty and wealth are both parts of the reality in this rainbow nation. As soon as you arrived in Cape Town, you noticed the diversity of the people of South Africa. They are a blend of colors, from the fairest white to the

The people of South Africa demonstrate hope
for the future even in the country's slums.

"When for the first time we voted in our millions, as equals—men and women of every color, language and religion; rich and poor—our nation was reborn."

—President Nelson Mandela, Freedom Day celebration, April 27, 1999[1]

darkest black and all shades in between. Some indigenous tribes have lived here for millennia, while others settled here several centuries ago. Some people trace their heritage to ancestors who came to South Africa to seek their fortune. Others came here to work the land and build the industries that have made South Africa the economic leader of the African continent.

For many years, South Africa's black majority and people of mixed race faced severe discrimination. The white minority made the laws, and everyone had to follow them. But that changed in 1994, when South Africa held its first free and fair election and became a true democracy.

Many of the world's largest diamonds have been found in South African mines.

South Africa is a young country. You can feel the energy and optimism of the people as you travel the streets of Cape Town. South Africa is a work in progress, but the basic foundations for success are in place. South Africans of all races, ethnicities, and religions are working hard to make this nation successful and to improve life for all of its citizens.

SNAPSHOT

Official name: Republic of South Africa

Capital cities: Pretoria (administrative), Cape Town (legislative), and Bloemfontein (judicial)

Form of government: republic, parliamentary system

Title of leader: president

Currency: rand

Population (July 2011 est.): 49,004,031
World rank: 25

Size: 470,693 square miles (1,219,090 sq km)
World Rank: 25

Languages: isiZulu, isiXhosa, Afrikaans, Sepedi, English, Setswana, Sesotho, Xitsonga, isiNdebele, Tshivenda, isiSwati

Official religion: none

Per capita GDP (2010, US dollars): $10,700
World Rank: 105

CHAPTER 2

GEOGRAPHY: NATURAL WONDERS

With mountains rising more than 10,000 feet (3,000 m), waterfalls cascading off cliffs, and miles of sandy beaches lining its shores, South Africa is a land of spectacular natural wonders. From river canyons to hot deserts, modern metropolises to sleepy fishing villages, this country is, above all, rich in its geographic diversity.

COASTLINE AND CLIMATE

South Africa's 1,836-mile (2,955-km) coastline is its dominant geographic feature.[1] Here, at the southern tip of Africa, two oceans meet: the Indian Ocean brings the warm waters of the Agulhas current from Mozambique, and the Atlantic Ocean brings the cold Benguela current,

South Africa's Tugela Falls is the second-highest waterfall in the world.

This lighthouse at Cape Agulhas prevents shipwrecks at the southernmost tip of Africa.

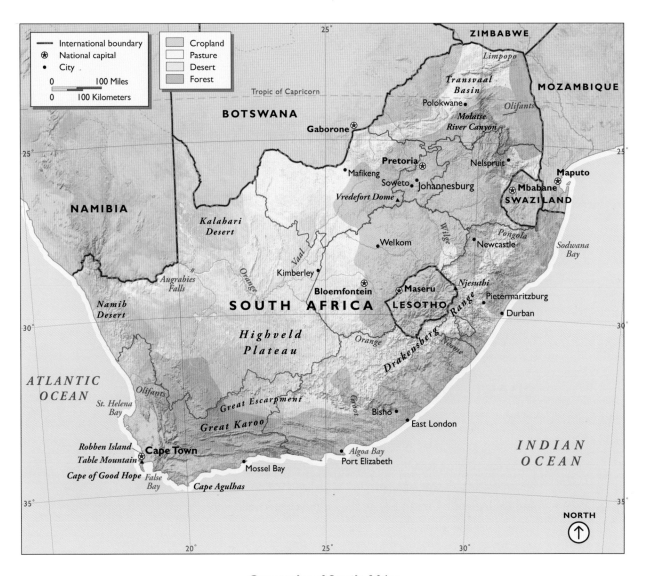

Geography of South Africa

which surges north from Antarctica. These cold and warm waters merge at the southernmost point in Africa—Cape Agulhas.

These ocean currents determine South Africa's climate. Along much of the western coast, the climate is dry and mild, similar to that of Southern California and the Mediterranean. Along the eastern coast, the climate is warm and humid, much like that in areas bordering the Gulf of Mexico. In the inner regions, the climate varies between these two extremes. Overall, the country enjoys mild weather, except in the harsh deserts in the northwest, near the border with Namibia. South Africa is located in the Southern Hemisphere, so its seasons are the opposite of those in Europe and North America. Winter lasts from June through September, and summer runs from December through March.

VREDEFORT DOME

The world's oldest meteor crater is located in South Africa, about 60 miles (100 km) from Johannesburg. When an asteroid hit the earth here 2 billion years ago, it left an impact area that was about 240 miles (380 km) across.[2] Although much of this area has since eroded away, the crater, called the Vredefort Dome, is still visible. It is considered one of the three largest impact craters in the world.

South Africa borders five countries: Botswana and Zimbabwe on the north, Namibia on the northwest, and Swaziland and Mozambique on the northeast. In addition, the mountain kingdom of Lesotho is surrounded on all sides by South

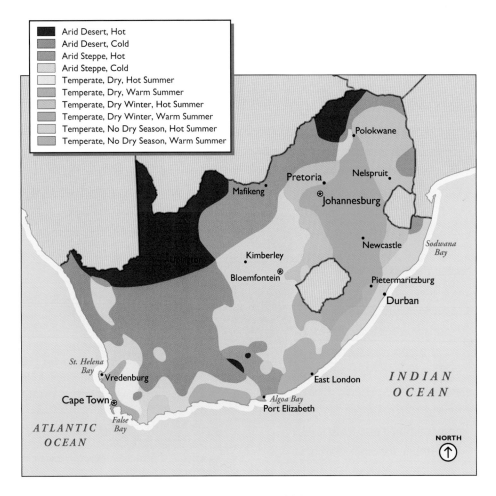

Climate of South Africa

Africa. Beyond the South African mainland, approximately 1,200 miles (1,900 km) offshore in the Atlantic Ocean, are two islands that are included in the nation's territory.

AVERAGE TEMPERATURE AND RAINFALL

Region (City)	Average January Temperature Minimum/ Maximum	Average July Temperature Minimum/Maximum	Average Rainfall: January/July
Eastern Interior (Johannesburg)	60/77°F (16/25°C)	42/61°F (6/16°C)	4.9/0.2 inches (12.5/0.5 cm)
Central (Bloemfontein)	59/88°F (15/31°C)	28/63°F (-2/17°C)	3.2/0.4 inches (8.1/1.0 cm)
Northwest (Upington)	57/104°F (14/40°C)	27/80°F (-3/27°C)	0.9/0.1 inches (2.3/0.3 cm)
Southwest Cape Province (Cape Town)	63/77°F (17/25°C)	47/62°F (8/17°C)	0.6/3.3 inches (1.5/8.4 cm)
Eastern Cape (Port Elizabeth)	64/77°F (18/25°C)	48/68°F (9/20°C)	1.4/1.9 inches (3.6/4.8 cm)
Eastern Coastlands (Durban)	72/81°F (22/27°C)	55/72°F (13/22°C)	4.7/1.3 inches (12.0/3.6 cm)[4]

South Africa is slightly less than twice the size of Texas. It covers 470,693 square miles (1,219,090 sq km), making it the ninth-largest country in Africa.[3] Worldwide, South Africa ranks twenty-fifth in area.

LAND FORMATIONS

Much of the African continent lies on a high plateau. This plateau ranges from the Sahara desert in the north all the way south until it reaches a land feature in South Africa known as the Great Escarpment. The escarpment dips dramatically through cliffs and mountains before plunging down toward the coast.

The Molatse River Canyon is the largest nonarid canyon in the world.

In eastern areas of South Africa, the escarpment includes the Drakensberg Mountains. The tallest peak in South Africa—Njesuthi, at 11,181 feet (3,408 m)—is located in this mountain range.[5] On rare occasions, it snows there. It features one of the world's deepest river canyons, the Molatse River Canyon (formerly known as the Blyde River Canyon). The Molatse River Canyon Nature Reserve is home to primates, crocodiles, hippopotamuses, waterbirds, and otters.

The inland plateau in South Africa is called the Highveld. (*Veld* is the Afrikaans word for "field.") Nearly two-thirds of South Africa's land is in the Highveld, as are the cities of Johannesburg, Pretoria, and Bloemfontein. The soil is rich, so many crops are grown there.

On the northeast, the boundary of the Highveld is marked by a rocky ridge known as the Witwatersrand. There, rich mineral deposits

The rushing waters of the Molatse River formed these potholes over many years.

WORLD HERITAGE SITES

The United Nations Educational, Scientific, and Cultural Organization (UNESCO) has identified 911 properties worldwide as having outstanding universal value and designated them as World Heritage sites. UNESCO encourages the identification, protection, and preservation of cultural and natural heritage sites around the world, due to their outstanding value to humanity. South Africa has a total of eight, including four cultural sites, three natural sites, and one mixed (cultural and natural) site:

• Simangaliso Wetland Park

• Robben Island

• Cradle of Humankind

• uKhahlamba Drakensberg Park

• Mapungubwe Cultural Landscape

• Cape Floral Region

• Vredefort Dome

• Richtersveld Cultural and Botanical Landscape

can be found deep below the earth's surface. Located there are many of South Africa's gold mines.

The Vaal and Orange Rivers run through the Highveld, and the Limpopo River forms the border between South Africa and Botswana and Zimbabwe. The Orange River is South Africa's longest, beginning in the Drakensberg Mountains, running through the Northern Cape, and ending at the Atlantic Ocean. Along the Orange River's 1,300-mile (2,100-km) path is Augrabies Falls, in the northwest near the Namibian border.[6]

Augrabies Falls

PROVINCES AND CITIES

South Africa has three capitals: Pretoria, Cape Town, and Bloemfontein. Different government functions are located in each city. The administrative capital and location of many government departments is Pretoria. Cape Town hosts the legislative branch, and Bloemfontein, the judicial capital, is home to the Supreme Court of Appeal.

South Africa is divided into nine provinces: KwaZulu-Natal, Eastern Cape, Western Cape, Northern Cape, Free State, North West, Gauteng, Limpopo, and Mpumalanga. Durban is the largest city in KwaZulu-Natal, and Pietermaritzburg is the provincial capital. This province is known for its beautiful beaches, warm weather, and sugarcane plantations. Its climate is subtropical, with wetlands, estuaries, and lush forests.

Port Elizabeth is home to the oldest British building in southern Africa, Fort Frederick.

Port Elizabeth is the largest city in Eastern Cape, and Bisho is the provincial capital. This province has a spectacular coastline and is famous for its incredible surfing. Inland areas are home to old-growth forests and the Karoo, a high, arid plateau.

As well as being one of the three national capitals, Cape Town is both the capital and largest city in Western Cape Province. This province is known for its growing wine

Aloe plants grow on the arid Karoo plateau.

industry, excellent fishing, and dramatic coastline, known as the Garden Route.

Kimberley is the capital and major city in the sparsely populated Northern Cape, the nation's largest province. This semiarid region has some of the most extreme weather in the country and is the home of South Africa's diamond-mining industry.

Bloemfontein, the largest city in Free State, is the provincial capital as well as one of the national capitals. Mining is critical to the state's economy. With its wide-open prairies, Free State is also the nation's agricultural center, producing goods ranging from asparagus to flowers to corn to sheep.

GARDEN ROUTE

One of South Africa's most beautiful regions, known as the Garden Route, stretches from Mossel Bay in the west to Port Elizabeth in the east. In this region, a thick evergreen forest meets a rocky coastline. Secluded beaches abound in this favorite vacation spot of South Africans. Garden Route National Park was created in 2009 to conserve the amazing biodiversity found in this region.

Mafikeng is the capital of North West Province. It is a rural area and has many types of mineral resources. Many people there are employed in the platinum, diamond, granite, and copper mines.

Gauteng Province's capital, Johannesburg, is also South Africa's largest city. This province is home to both rich and poor, skyscrapers and shanties. Jo'burg, as South Africans call it, is the economic engine of the nation. Pretoria, also in Gauteng, is one of the three national capitals.

Polokwane, formerly called Pietersburg, is the provincial capital of Limpopo. This region is characterized by bushveld, a habitat that includes trees and grasslands. Limpopo is a rural farming and ranching region. Kruger National Park, the most famous animal reserve in South Africa and one of the nation's major tourist destinations, is located there.

Nelspruit is the provincial capital of Mpumalanga. This province has beautiful natural scenery, including rolling hills, deep ravines, dense forests, and thundering waterfalls. The main industries are mining and sugarcane and citrus fruit farming.

LIMPOPO RIVER

In *Just So Stories*, published in 1902, British author Rudyard Kipling included a tale called "The Elephant's Child." In this fantasy, a young elephant wanders down to the bank of the Limpopo River to learn what the crocodile is having for dinner. The crocodile grabs onto the elephant's previously "boot-sized" nose, stretching it out during a long tug of war. According to Kipling, this is how the elephant got its trademark long trunk. Today, the Limpopo River in South Africa is still home to elephants, crocodiles, hippos, and many other majestic animals.

CHAPTER 3

ANIMALS AND NATURE: A LAND OF BIODIVERSITY

South Africa occupies only 2 percent of the world's land but is home to 10 percent of the world's plant species and 7 percent of its species of mammals, reptiles, and birds. Along the nation's coastlines, 15 percent of the world's marine species can be seen.[1] Many of these animals are found nowhere else on Earth.

South Africa has the third-highest level of biodiversity of any country. The Cape Peninsula alone contains a greater variety of plant species than can be found in all of the United Kingdom. Ten percent of the world's flowering plant species grow in South Africa.

Not only does South Africa have many types of animals and plants, it also has some of the most majestic. Nearly 300 species of mammals can be found here. The famous "Big Five" are what many tourists want

South Africa's oceans are rich with biodiversity.

THE SPRINGBOK

The springbok, a fast-running and high-jumping gazelle, is the national animal of South Africa. But it has even greater significance as the namesake and symbol of the national rugby team. In 1995, the Springboks made it to the Rugby World Cup, which was held in South Africa. At the time, a campaign was underway to change the name of the team to the Proteas in recognition of the national flower. For many black South Africans, the springbok was a reminder of the apartheid government, which had placed the image of a springbok on the back of the Krugerrand gold coin and on postage stamps. As a gesture of reconciliation to rugby fans, the majority of whom were white, President Nelson Mandela intervened to maintain the Springbok name. The team went on to win the final championship game, and all of its citizens—blacks and whites—were united in celebration. This story formed the basis of the 2009 film *Invictus*.

to see: the lion, rhinoceros, elephant, Cape buffalo, and leopard. Some of the other famous land animals native to South Africa include the giraffe, crocodile, hyena, cheetah, warthog, eland, hippopotamus, zebra, and the springbok, South Africa's national animal.

Visitors to South Africa can have the rare experience of seeing wildlife in its natural habitat, living together in family groups and gathering around watering holes. But, the days of seeing massive herds of animals roaming the Highveld are long gone.

South Africa also has an amazing variety of life in the sea. Great white sharks, orcas, southern right whales, turtles, blue whales, and humpback dolphins all live in the waters along the nation's coasts. Divers and snorkelers can

Two springboks fight for dominance.

see an incredible assortment of tropical fish in the coral reefs that line the coast of the Indian Ocean near Sodwana Bay. The Atlantic coast is a prime fishing area and a great place to spot many kinds of migrating whales.

PLANTS

The Cape Floral Kingdom, a UNESCO World Heritage site, is a series of eight protected areas that has been called "the world's hottest hot-spot" for plant diversity.[2] A great diversity of botanical life is concentrated here, representing nearly 20 percent of all flora species found in Africa. Many kinds of orchids, lilies, irises, agapanthus, and pelargoniums grow in abundance here.

South Africa has several iconic plants, including the legendary baobab tree; halfmen plants, which look like a human from a distance; and the national flower, the King Protea, a beautiful and hardy pincushion-like flower that is found in a range of colors.

PENGUINS

A colony of 3,000 penguins can be seen on Boulders Beach, not far from Cape Town. Boardwalks crisscross the beach where the penguins come ashore, allowing visitors close-up views. Climate change has been blamed for the dwindling number of penguins here. This animal was added to the endangered species list in 2010.

Pink proteas, South Africa's national flower

A LEGACY OF CONSERVATION

Through strict conservation programs, South Africa has managed to preserve many species and even bring back a few from the brink of extinction. This has been done through practicing conservation and establishing animal reserves. The first reserve, the Sabie Game Reserve, was established in 1898 in what was called the Transvaal Republic. The name of the reserve was later changed to Kruger National Park to honor former president Paul Kruger, who proposed creating it.

Since the founding of Kruger National Park, 19 other national parks have been established across the country, but in terms of diversity, Kruger is still the greatest of them all. Within its vast boundaries, hundreds of different species can be found, including 507 birds, 336 trees, 147 mammals, 114 reptiles, 49 fish, and 34 amphibians.[3] During daylight

BAOBAB TREES

According to San legend, the baobab tree offended God, so he planted it upside down. This tale probably originated because of the tree's odd appearance. It has a thick, gnarled trunk and small, rootlike branches. Baobabs are among the longest-living trees in the world. One tree in Limpopo Province has been estimated to be 6,000 years old. In the drought-prone areas where these trees are found, they provide an important source of food and shelter for animals.

This baobab tree is protected in Kruger National Park.

PRIVATE GAME RESERVES

In addition to South Africa's national parks, private game reserves have been established. Some of these have been created for the purpose of preserving animals, but others have been created purely for the enjoyment of hunters. In 2008, the most recent year for which records are available, 1,050 lions were killed by hunters who paid to shoot an animal in an enclosed area of a private game reserve.[4] These lions were born and raised in captivity for the sole purpose of becoming hunting trophies. The South African government licenses the practice, welcomes the revenue, and calls it a "sustainable utilization of natural resources."[5] The Professional Hunters Association of South Africa reported that 16,394 foreign hunters killed more than 46,000 animals in the year ending September 2007, including elephants, rhinos, and giraffes.[6]

hours, visitors can drive around Kruger's 5 million acres (2 million ha) to view animals. Then in the evening, they can set up camp or stay in one of the park's lodges. Control of some of these establishments has been transferred to the indigenous peoples, allowing them to receive financial benefits from tourism in their ancestral homelands.

Pollution, overfishing, and the use of shark nets have all been blamed for the declining populations of some marine species. Whaling was a major industry in the nineteenth century, and the southern right whale was the main target until it was nearly wiped out. Since this majestic creature became a protected animal in South African waters in 1935, its population has increased.

Conservation is an urgent issue in South Africa because many of the nation's species have already been identified as threatened. Included are 15 percent of the nation's plant species, 14 percent of its birds, 24 percent of its reptiles, 18 percent of its amphibians, 37 percent of its mammals, and 22 percent of its butterfly species.[7] Among the creatures critically endangered are the Cape parrot, the loggerhead sea turtle, the riverine rabbit, and the wattled crane.

POACHING

The combination of majestic wildlife and desperate poverty has resulted in the poaching of

ENDANGERED SPECIES IN SOUTH AFRICA

According to the International Union for Conservation of Nature (IUCN), South Africa is home to the following numbers of species that are categorized by the organization as Critically Endangered, Endangered, or Vulnerable:

Mammals	24
Birds	39
Reptiles	21
Amphibians	20
Fishes	81
Mollusks	21
Other Invertebrates	138
Plants	92
Total	441[8]

some of South Africa's most treasured and iconic animals. The rhinoceros is South Africa's most sought-after animal, due to the mistaken belief that ingesting powdered rhino horn has health benefits for humans. There is a high demand for rhino horn in China, Korea, and Vietnam, even though importation has been banned around the world. Rhino horn powder sells on the black market for up to $30,000 per pound, making it almost as valuable as gold. A single horn weighs approximately eight pounds (3.6 kg).

South Africa is currently losing one rhino to poachers almost every day, with more than 333 killed in 2010. At the beginning of 2011, there were an estimated 1,678 black rhinos and 19,400 white rhinos in South Africa, both on an upward population trend.[9] However, the encouraging population growth is threatened by increasing poaching. The surge in poaching has resulted in increased patrols and penalties against poachers, but some conservation activists fear these measures will not deter the criminals. Some animal groups have called for dehorning rhinos to take away poachers' incentive for killing them.

South Africa is home to one of Earth's smallest mammals, the least dwarf shrew.

Rhinoceroses are threatened by poaching.

CHAPTER 4

HISTORY: A COMPLICATED PAST

Africa is considered the birthplace of humanity. Archeologists have found well-preserved bones from early human ancestors across southern Africa. Many examples of a very early human relative, *Australopithecus africanus*, have been found in South African caves—some as old as 3 million years. An early example of modern humans, *Homo sapiens*, lived 100,000 years ago in what is today South Africa. Their bones and tools have been found, along with their cave paintings.

Among the tribes to inhabit the area were the San, also known as Bushmen. These people were hunters and gatherers, so they moved around to find food and water rather than living in one place. They recorded their way of life in rock paintings. Another early group of

Australopithecine skull found in South Africa

SAN CAVE PAINTINGS

The San people have been creating their art for at least 27,000 years, and it can be found in caves and rock overhangs all over South Africa. Archaeologists recently decoded the meanings of many of these paintings and found evidence that the people and animals in them symbolize the spiritual beliefs and customs of the San people. Visitors can view more than 40,000 rock art images at the uKhahlamba-Drakensberg Park in the KwaZulu-Natal Province.

people living in South Africa were the Khoikhoi. They were hunters and gatherers who later adapted to keeping cattle.

Beginning at least 1,700 years ago, groups of people speaking Bantu languages from the northern parts of the African continent began migrating south. They brought with them more sophisticated means of farming and hunting and made tools of metal. Both the Khoikhoi and the San people had lighter skin and were generally smaller in stature than the Bantu-speaking people.

EARLY EUROPEAN CONTACT

In 1488, Portuguese explorer Bartholomeu Dias was looking for a sea route from Europe to India when he became the first European to round the southern tip of Africa. The Europeans and Khoikhoi traded with each other, and their relationship was mostly friendly during the early days. Soon, the Dutch and the British sent ships to the area as well.

In 1652, the Dutch East India Company established a trading post at
Cape Town, and it became a busy port. The Dutch East India Company
had forbidden the enslavement of the indigenous people at the Cape
Colony. But in 1657, the first slaves were imported from other parts of
Africa and from Asia to help build the colony and work the fields.

Africa
do mappamundi de
Juan de la Cosa
piloto de
Christovaô colombo
era 1493 desenhado em 1500

The Khoikhoi and San were not enslaved because the Europeans needed to trade with them. Over the next century, however, most of the Khoikhoi and San populations were wiped out—some through battles with the Dutch but mostly through exposure to European diseases.

During the eighteenth century, more Dutch settlers came, as did other immigrants from France and Germany. These white settlers became known as the Boers, which means "farmers." Also during this period, a large number of slaves were imported. By 1717, half the population of the Cape Colony was slaves. Mixed marriages produced a new racial group that the Dutch came to refer to as "coloured." The racial divisions that would become significant in South Africa's future were now in place. The Dutch-ruled colony practiced discrimination against all nonwhite people.

In 1806, the British took over control of the Cape Colony, and in 1834, they abolished slavery throughout the British Empire. Shortly thereafter, a group of approximately 12,000 Boers embarked on what became known as the Great Trek. Called the Voortrekkers or the Trek Boers, they left areas ruled by the British to establish their own republics—the Orange Free State and the Transvaal—which they hoped would be white-ruled nations.

European-made map of Africa, 1500 CE

Zulu warriors, 1875

FIGHTING OVER RESOURCES

Throughout the nineteenth century, battles erupted between the European settlers and different Bantu-speaking tribes, including the Xhosa, Zulu, Sotho, and Matabele. The Bantu-speaking tribes also fought against each other, as did the various European groups.

One of the most famous battles, the Battle of Blood River in 1838, was fought between approximately 500 Boers and 10,000 Zulus. An estimated 3,000 Zulus were killed there—so many that the blood of the dead turned the Ncome River red. Although the Boers were outnumbered, they won that battle, and after 1879, the Zulus were no longer considered a great army.

By the end of the nineteenth century, the British controlled the Cape

SHAKA AND THE ZULUS

Most historians agree that the greatest king of the Zulus was Shaka, who ruled from 1816 to 1828. Under Shaka, the Zulus were the most powerful army in Africa. Shaka trained his warriors in new ways of fighting and equipped them with better weapons. He also imposed harsh discipline on his warriors, making them train heavily and go barefoot to toughen up their feet. Because of their superior military tactics, the Zulu army was victorious in many battles. It increased its influence across southern Africa, capturing the land and cattle of many other tribes. Shaka's legacy is still strong, and he is regarded by many Zulus today as their greatest king. In 2010, the new international airport in Durban was named after Shaka.

Paul Kruger led South Africa from 1883 to 1900.

and Natal colonies and the Boers had won control over the inland areas of the Transvaal and the Orange Free State, which came to be known as the Boer republics. The Transvaal elected Paul Kruger as president in 1883. Kruger implemented a policy of white supremacy, which denied blacks many rights. The Boers believed they were a superior race and that blacks should be their servants. Their beliefs could be traced back to the teachings of the Dutch Reformed Church and the theology of Calvinism.

The battle for control of South Africa only intensified after the discovery of diamonds in the region of Kimberley in 1867 and the discovery of gold in the area near Johannesburg in 1886. In 1871, the British took over the diamond fields. Many people from around the world rushed in to stake their claims. Tensions grew between the British and the Boers, and in 1899, the Anglo-Boer War began. Vastly outnumbered, the Boers were defeated by the British in 1902.

Although some black South Africans fought alongside the Boers, most of them supported the British during the Anglo-Boer War. Blacks believed they had a better chance to gain more civil rights and land under British rule. In 1910, Great Britain approved the South Africa Act, creating the Union of South Africa—comprised of the Orange Free State, Transvaal, and the Cape and Natal Provinces—and taking away the political rights of blacks. The nation became an independent dominion of the British Commonwealth, an association of former British colonies. After the war, the British gave in to many of the Boers' demands, and over the next several decades, black freedom became more and more restricted.

BLACKS LOSE THEIR RIGHTS

In 1913, blacks lost their right to buy land anywhere except those areas set aside for them in the Natives' Land Act. Even though blacks made up 80 percent of South Africa's population, they were allowed to own an area comprising approximately 7 percent of the country, later increased to 13 percent.[1] The lands set aside for blacks were the worst places for farms and had few natural resources. Other race-based laws soon followed, governing which jobs people of different races could hold. The mixed-race people known as coloureds also faced restrictions, as did Indians and other Asians.

The Kimberley mine is the largest hand-dug hole on Earth.

Resistance to these policies began right away. In 1912, a predecessor was formed to the group that would eventually be called the African National Congress (ANC). The group organized labor strikes to increase pay and improve working conditions for blacks. The group also tried to negotiate with the British government but made little progress.

White women could not vote in South Africa until 1930.

The white government of South Africa created a system that institutionalized racism, making blacks second-class citizens in their own country. The Boers, now increasingly called Afrikaners, used some of the teachings of the Dutch Reformed Church to justify this system. They interpreted several Old Testament Bible verses to mean that whites are racially superior to all others. The white government's system of racial separation came to be known as apartheid, which means "separateness" in the Afrikaans language. Although whites benefited from this system, not all of them agreed with it. The system was implemented after 1948.

Beginning in 1952, all blacks over the age of 16 had to carry a pass wherever they went, and they were allowed in white areas only as part of their work. Authorities checked these passes and arrested blacks who broke the pass law. These so-called pass laws became a symbol of apartheid and sparked massive protests.

Students demonstrating against the South African government, 1977

THE RESISTANCE MOVEMENT

From the beginning of apartheid, there were people from across South African society—blacks and whites—who disagreed with the system. But the system continued because only whites could vote and the majority of white voters wanted to keep the advantages they gained under apartheid.

The daily lives of South Africans who were not white grew more difficult. Blacks who were known to belong to the ANC or other protest groups were rounded up and jailed under false charges. Blacks were not allowed to ride buses, trains, or planes with whites, and very few blacks went to school past the elementary level.

In 1955, leaders of the resistance movement created a declaration of principles called the

STEVEN BIKO

Steven Biko was a black student who became a political activist in the late 1960s and encouraged other blacks to protest against the apartheid system. Biko founded the Black Consciousness Movement, which ignited a sense of pride among blacks and encouraged young blacks to join together to fight against the injustices forced on them. In 1973, the government declared Biko a banned person, which meant he could no longer speak in front of groups or leave his hometown. After being jailed in 1977, he died, and many believe his death was the result of torture by his captors. Biko's death led to an unprecedented level of outrage, not only among the estimated 10,000 to 20,000 people who mourned him at his funeral but across the globe. The death of Biko caught the world's attention, and from that point on, the outside pressure on South Africa to end its racial policies increased dramatically.

Freedom Charter, which advocated equal rights for all people. The government responded by putting Mandela and 155 others on trial for high treason in 1956, but they were acquitted for lack of evidence.

In 1960, thousands of unarmed South Africans participated in a protest organized by the Pan Africanist Congress (PAC). When the demonstrators gathered to protest the unjust pass laws at the police station in Sharpeville, the police opened fire. More than 200 people were injured and 69 died. After the government banned the ANC and PAC, some political activists turned to armed struggle to change the apartheid system.

FREEDOM CHARTER

The Freedom Charter was written and signed by members of the resistance movement in 1955:

"We, the People of South Africa, declare for all our country and the world to know:

that South Africa belongs to all who live in it, black and white, and that no government can justly claim authority unless it is based on the will of all the people;

that our people have been robbed of their birthright to land, liberty and peace by a form of government founded on injustice and inequality;

that our country will never be prosperous or free until all our people live in brotherhood, enjoying equal rights and opportunities;

that only a democratic state, based on the will of all the people, can secure to all their birthright without distinction of colour, race, sex or belief;

And therefore, we, the people of South Africa, black and white together equals, countrymen and brothers adopt this Freedom Charter.

And we pledge ourselves to strive together, sparing neither strength nor courage, until the democratic changes here set out have been won."[2]

The South African government reacted to strikes, demonstrations, and protests by banning the organizations that led them, including the ANC and the PAC. The leaders of these organizations were jailed or forced into exile. One of those leaders was a lawyer named Nelson Rolihlahla Mandela. Mandela worked within the ANC's Youth League to oppose the apartheid rules and advocate for a democratic South Africa.

In 1961, South Africa declared itself an independent republic and created its own currency, flag, and national anthem. Soon, it left the British Commonwealth, where it had been condemned and isolated for its apartheid policy.

ROBBEN ISLAND

During the apartheid era, political prisoners were sent to Robben Island, several miles offshore from Cape Town. The island was used as a prison in colonial days, as well. Nelson Mandela spent approximately 18 of his 27 years in prison at Robben Island. It has been preserved as a reminder of the apartheid era and is now one of South Africa's top tourist destinations.

In 1962, Mandela and several other ANC leaders were arrested again and found guilty of sabotaging the government. This time, they were convicted and eventually sentenced to life in prison.

With the resistance leaders in jail or in exile, the government continued its crackdown. Police and military forces frequently battled protesters in the streets to suppress their efforts. In 1970, the United Nations General Assembly described apartheid as a crime against the conscience and dignity of humanity. In 1976, South African police killed 600 people by some estimates during protests in Soweto Township, outside Johannesburg.[3]

ISOLATED FROM THE WORLD

An international movement to make South Africa change its apartheid laws began. The International Olympic Committee barred South Africa from competing in the Olympic Games, and other sports and cultural organizations issued similar rulings. Across the United States in the 1970s and 1980s, college students held campus demonstrations against apartheid and called for the US government and US corporations to stop doing business with South Africa. Famous musicians wrote songs about Mandela, shining a spotlight on the world's most famous political prisoner.

Under apartheid, the police had the right to use violence or kill and to hold people without trial.

Within South Africa, people were arrested or banned for writing newspaper articles, plays, poems, songs, or books criticizing the government and its policies. Many South Africans of all races disagreed with the government's policies, and some decided to leave the country to organize opposition to the apartheid system in other countries.

Many nations imposed economic sanctions on South Africa, and the nation's economy faltered, despite its significant mineral wealth.

Nelson Mandela celebrates with his supporters on April 21, 1994, days before winning the presidential election.

In response, President P. W. Botha made a few minor concessions to try to relieve the international boycotts. But by this time, international opinion was firmly against South Africa, and the world demanded that the apartheid system be completely dismantled.

A new leader came to power in South Africa in 1989, and he knew the days of white supremacy had to end. Shortly after F. W. de Klerk was sworn in as South Africa's president, he announced that he would lift the bans on the ANC and other resistance groups, allow more freedom of the press, and release the political prisoners.

A NEW NATION

The weather in Cape Town was warm and sunny on February 11, 1990. But the weather was not the reason people were dancing in the streets. Not just Cape Town but the entire country of South Africa was in a state of euphoria that day, because after spending 27 years in prison, Nelson Mandela had been set free. This historic day set South Africa on a new path.

At Cape Town's city hall, 50,000 people waited for hours in the midsummer sun to listen to Mandela's first public speech. He told the jubilant crowd, "Our struggle has reached a decisive moment. . . . Our march to freedom is irreversible."[4]

Nelson Mandela's prison number, 46664, is now the name of an HIV/AIDS awareness organization.

Mandela soon began negotiations with the white government to lead the country through a peaceful transition to a true multiracial democracy. International sanctions that had punished South Africa for its apartheid laws for 30 years were lifted. But building a new nation would not be easy. With the society and its structure in flux, many people grew worried and impatient about what the new South Africa would be like. Violence in the streets increased dramatically. A struggle developed among the Zulu Inkatha Freedom Party, the ANC, and other political parties to determine which group would lead the country into the future.

Nelson Mandela was born on July 18, 1918.

The first democratic election was held on April 27, 1994. Long lines formed across South Africa, as people who had been denied the right to vote now exercised this new and hard-fought freedom. Many people expressed joy and felt vindicated after their long struggle. "I just voted the racists out of power," said Koni Mabandla.[5] "I think the fact that I'm able to vote for Nelson Mandela is the best day of my life, short of the births of my kids and my wedding day," said Marlene Davis.[6]

The ANC won the election with more than 62 percent of the vote, and Mandela was sworn in as president of South Africa on May 9, 1994.[7] He spoke about the challenge of building a new nation, establishing a peaceful coexistence among the races, and reconciling the sins of the past. South Africans now celebrate April 27 as a national holiday called Freedom Day.

Since the ending of apartheid and the beginning of a new democracy in South Africa, the international community has reestablished friendly relations with the African nation. Internally, the wounds of apartheid are slow to heal. The Mandela administration set up the Truth and Reconciliation Commission, which sought to expose and prosecute apartheid-era violence and other rights abuses. The country has also faced the challenges of educating its people, improving its infrastructure and economy, and fighting some of the highest infection rates of HIV/AIDS in the world.

CHAPTER 5
PEOPLE: MIXED HERITAGE

South Africa is a land of abundance that has drawn people for centuries. Its strategic location at the southern tip of the continent, temperate climate, plentiful animal and plant life, and rich mineral resources have brought together many groups of people. The San and Khoikhoi sometimes clashed, but they also traded and intermarried with each other. And in addition to the white immigrants who wanted land for farming, grazing, housing, and mining, many black peoples came from other parts of Africa seeking to expand their tribal areas. Today in South Africa, there are very few people who can trace their ancestors back to the Khoikhoi and San tribes.

The San and the Khoikhoi are sometimes referred to collectively as Bushmen.

This man is one of the few who belong to the San tribe today.

YOU SAY IT!

English	Zulu	Xhosa	Afrikaans
Good morning/Hello	Sawubona (sah-woo-BOH-nah)	Molo (MOH-loh)	Hallo (hah-LOH)
Good-bye	Hamba kahle (HAHM-bah GAH-hlay)	Hamba kakuhle (HAHM-bah gah-GOO-hlay)	Tot siens (toht-SEENS)
Thank you	Ngiyabonga (ihn-gee-yah-BONE-gah	Enkosi (ihn-KOHS)	Dankei (DAHN-kee)
Please	Ngiyakucela (ihn-gee-yah-k!oo-SAY-lah)	Nceda (ihn-S!AY-dah)	Assblief (ah-say-BLEEF)

The Zulu and Xhosa languages include clicking sounds made with the tongue, indicated by an exclamation point.

A MIXING OF PEOPLE

In 2010, the South African government estimated the country's population at 49,991,300.[1] The majority of modern South Africans are descendents of Bantu-speaking people who originated in Nigeria. These tribes began establishing themselves in South Africa around the fourth century CE, according to archaeological finds. The Zulu, Xhosa, Ndebele, Swazi, Sotho, Tswana, and Venda tribes all have long histories in South Africa. The nation has 11 official languages, nine of which are African.

Woman and sons wearing traditional Zulu
clothing, Lesedi Cultural Village

LANGUAGES OF SOUTH AFRICA

IsiZulu: 23.8%

IsiXhosa: 17.6%

Afrikaans: 13.3%

Sepedi: 9.4%

English: 8.2%

Setswana: 8.2%

Sesotho: 7.9%

Xitsonga: 4.4%

Other: 7.2%[4]

In 2010, there were an estimated 39.68 million blacks descended from Bantu-speaking peoples in South Africa, comprising 79.4 percent of the population. The white population of South Africa was 4.58 million, or 9.2 percent of the population.[2] Included in this population are people who trace their ancestors to the Afrikaner, or Boer, settlers who arrived in the seventeenth century, as well as people with British ancestors. Because of intermarriage over the years, there are also many families who can claim both heritages or some other European ancestry.

The so-called coloured population resulted from the intermarriage of people from different ethnic groups. Most of this population is concentrated in the Cape Province. In 2010, approximately 4.42 million South Africans belonged to this ethnic group, comprising 8.8 percent of the national population.[3] A subgroup of the coloured population is the Cape Malays, a group of Indonesian immigrants who are descendents of slaves brought to work at the Cape Colony. Indians and Asians make up the smallest major ethnic group in South Africa. In 2010, they numbered 1.29 million people, or 2.6 percent of the overall population.[5] Indians are concentrated in KwaZulu-Natal, near the city of Durban.

South Africa is a young nation in more than one way. It is a new country and a new democracy, but it is also heavily populated with young people. Out of a total population of approximately 50 million people, nearly one-third are under the age of 15, and half the nation is 25 or younger. The population's general life expectancy is 49 years, which ranks 215th in the world.[6]

CITIES AND REGIONS

Many South Africans live in the large cities of Johannesburg, Cape Town, and Durban. Gauteng Province is smallest in size but largest in population. Gauteng includes the cities of Johannesburg and Pretoria, plus their townships and outlying suburbs, and has a

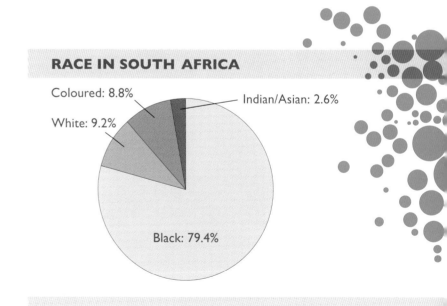

RACE IN SOUTH AFRICA

Coloured: 8.8%

Indian/Asian: 2.6%

White: 9.2%

Black: 79.4%

**Moses Mabhida stadium in Durban,
one of South Africa's largest cities**

population of 11.19 million. Western Cape Province, which includes Cape Town, has 5.22 million residents. KwaZulu-Natal has a population of 10.64 million.[7]

More than half of South Africans—an estimated 61 percent—now live in and around cities.[8] In the past, many blacks were forced to relocate to homelands according to which tribe their ancestors came from. After the dismantling of apartheid, many people left these homelands, also known as Bantustans. This migration from the countryside to the cities has been a growing trend, as people have come to cities to seek employment and a better life. But this trend has meant that the population density in South Africa's cities is very high. Millions of people have settled into the areas designated as black townships outside the major cities. Soweto (short for South West Township),

AFRICAN HOMELANDS DURING APARTHEID

In 1959, the apartheid government began to create homelands, or Bantustans, which were set aside for blacks. Each tribe, or nation, had its own designated territory. The government told the black people they were now citizens of these homelands. Some blacks were forcibly removed from areas where they had lived for generations and relocated to one of these rural Bantustans. The names of the homelands were KwaZulu, Transkei, Ciskei, Venda, Bophuthatswana, KwaNdebele, KaNgwane, Qwaqwa, Lebowa, and Gazankulu. The Bantustans were abolished in 1994 with the adoption of the new constitution.

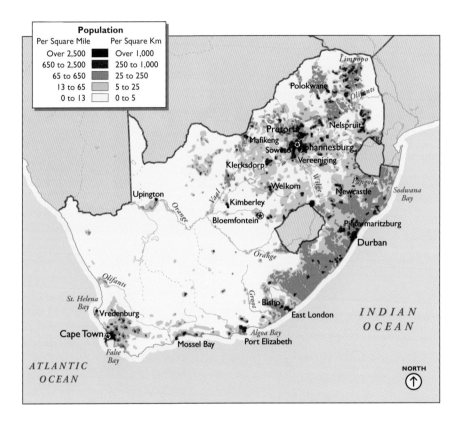

Population Density of South Africa

outside Johannesburg, has an official population of approximately 1.3 million people, though many estimate the actual population is much higher.[9]

Aerial view of the sprawling slum of Soweto

RELIGIONS

South Africa's new constitution guarantees religious freedom for all. Its people hold a wide range of beliefs, but nearly 80 percent identify themselves as Christian. Islam has the second-largest number of followers, with 1.5 percent, and Hindu is next, with 1.2 percent. Less than 1 percent of South Africans report themselves to be Jewish, African traditionalist, or other, and 15 percent say they hold no religious beliefs.[10]

There is some crossover between the different spiritual groups. Many blacks, in particular, incorporate some traditional African beliefs into their Christian identity. For example, the custom of slaughtering an animal when a young person comes of age is still commonly practiced in many African cultures. Paying respect to one's ancestors through ancient rituals is a central belief in traditional African culture.

TRADITIONAL HEALERS

Many Africans turn to traditional healers to help them when they are sick. An *inyanga* is someone who knows the healing power of plants and herbs and can prescribe remedies to cure a person's illness. A healer called an *isangoma* acts as an intermediary between a person and his or her ancestors. The *isangoma* consults with the spirits to find out what is wrong and then directs the sick person to perform rituals that will please the ancestors and thereby bring about healing.

An isangoma in her workroom

CHAPTER 6
CULTURE: THE RAINBOW NATION

South Africa has been nicknamed the "rainbow nation" because of its many different spiritual and racial backgrounds, forms of art, foods, and traditions. With such a diversity of people in one country, there is not one culture but many. Even so, South Africans also have their own unique customs.

TRADITIONAL CRAFTS, ART, MUSIC, AND DANCE

Traditional arts such as beading, ceramics, embroidery, basket making, and weaving flourish today, aided by the tourism industry. Crafters sell their items in street markets and on roadsides all over South Africa. The San people, for example, produce paintings in the tradition of the rock art

Graffiti on a wall in Durban shows aspects of South African culture.

ISICATHAMIYA

Isicathamiya is a type of singing made famous by the group Ladysmith Black Mambazo. The group performed on US music star Paul Simon's 1986 album *Graceland*, which brought them worldwide fame. Isicathamiya has roots in Zulu tradition, apartheid-era labor camps, and gospel music, and it is performed by choirs all across South Africa. The sound track to the Disney film *The Lion King* also features isicathamiya singing. Isicathamiya choirs are usually comprised entirely of men and are often sung without musical accompaniment.

that their ancestors created centuries ago. The Ndebele are known for painting brightly colored patterns on their homes. During the apartheid era, painters and sculptors of different racial backgrounds began a genre of resistance art, which became a popular form of self-expression.

South Africa also has a vibrant music scene. Many types of music can be heard in clubs, in concert halls, and on street corners. Among the world-famous South African musicians are Johnny Clegg, Hugh Masekela, Miriam Makeba, and the group Ladysmith Black Mambazo. South Africa has created some of its own unique forms of music and adapted others. *Kwaito* is a uniquely South African blend of hip-hop, dance, reggae, and rap music that has emerged in the past few decades. It is a part of the black township culture and is often sung in a kind of street slang called *Tsotsitaal* or *Isicamtho*.

Africa has a long tradition of self-expression through dance, and spontaneous public dance celebrations are not unusual. A uniquely

Isicathamiya singing group Ladysmith Black Mambazo

African dance march known as the *Toyi-Toyi* has long been used as a form of protest. During the apartheid era, hundreds of people often joined in this massive street dance.

Gumboot dancing began in the gold mines of South Africa during the apartheid era. It takes its name from the rubber rain boots known as "gum boots" that were the standard footwear of miners. Black mine workers were not allowed to talk to each other while they worked and were often chained together at the ankles. Dancing was a way for them to communicate. Gumboot dance troupes now perform in dance shows and on the streets.

In 2006, the film *Tsotsi* won the Academy Award for Best Foreign Language Film.

Another form of dance that has gained popularity in South Africa is Afro-Fusion. It blends African ritual and dance with Western contemporary dance and ballet. New dance companies have sprouted up all over South Africa. These emerging artists have found success both at home and on stages around the world.

HOLIDAYS AND FESTIVALS

South Africa has 12 annual public holidays, including New Year's Day, Good Friday, Workers Day, and Christmas Day. The other eight holidays are unique to South Africa and celebrate the country's diverse people, heritage, and history. Human Rights Day is held each year on March 21 to commemorate the day when peaceful protesters were killed by police in Sharpeville in 1960. South Africans celebrate Family Day every year on

Thousands of church members travel on pilgrimage
to a holy site in the Drakensberg Mountains, 2008.

the Monday after Easter. April 27, the day of the first free and fair election in South Africa in 1994, is now a national holiday. Youth Day is celebrated each year on June 16, marking the start of the Soweto uprising in 1976, when police shot at black schoolchildren protesting the use of Afrikaans in schools. National Women's Day is August 9, the day a group of women in Pretoria marched to protest the pass laws in 1956. Heritage Day, when South Africans celebrate their collected history and culture, is September 24. December 16 is Reconciliation Day, and December 26 is the Day of Goodwill.

RECONCILIATION DAY

December 16 has long been a significant day in South Africa. Afrikaners used to call it the Day of the Vow to commemorate the Battle of Blood River, when they defeated the Zulus and made a promise to God to build a church if they were victorious. However, racial division was created by commemorating a day when many black Africans lost their lives. In 1995, President Nelson Mandela asked South Africans to reconcile their past conflicts and thus changed the holiday's focus.

Christmas is a big holiday in South Africa, just as it is in most of the Northern Hemisphere. But in the Southern Hemisphere, Christmas is a summer holiday and falls at the end of the school year, so children are off school for four or five weeks. Many families head off on a camping trip to the beach to enjoy some sunshine. A number of British Christmas traditions, which were brought to South Africa when it was a British colony, have carried on to the present time. People sing carols, decorate Christmas trees, and hang wreaths and stockings by the fire in anticipation of a visit from Father Christmas. Families exchange gifts, and many go to church for a service, returning home later for a traditional Christmas dinner.

FOOD

South African cuisine has been influenced by waves of immigrants who brought their own specialties with them. A typical meal includes some kind of meat or fish, as both are plentiful here. *Mealie pap*, a corn or grain porridge, is a staple of most black Africans' diets.

South Africans love to have a *braai*, or barbeque, at which they eat all kinds and all parts of animals, even zebra, ostrich, and antelope. A popular dish called walkie-talkies is grilled chicken feet and heads. Sausages called *boerewors* are quite popular and can be found everywhere. A popular snack is *biltong,* which is similar to beef jerky but can be made out of almost any kind of meat.

Indian food strongly influences South Africa's cuisine, especially in and around Durban, where there is a large Indian population. Spice markets there carry dozens of varieties of curries. Cape Town has a large Malayan minority, so Malayan cuisine is very popular. A favorite Malayan dish is *bobotie*, a meatloaf made with raisins, egg, banana, and chutney. Chinese, Indian, and European restaurants are also common in South African cities.

SPORTS

South Africans are crazy about soccer, rugby, and cricket—all sports imported from Europe. The nation's rugby team, the Springboks, has won the Rugby World Cup twice, in 1995 and 2007. The nation's cricket team is called the Proteas, and its soccer team is called Bafana Bafana, Zulu for "our boys."

Since South Africa's reentry into the world of international sports competition after the 1994 elections, it has become the first African nation to host several major sporting events, including the soccer, rugby, and cricket world cups. South African athletes now compete in the Olympic Games and other international competitions.

College-level rugby match in Bloemfontein, 2010

SOCCER'S WORLD CUP 2010

South Africa had the world's attention from June 11 to July 11, 2010, as the host of the FIFA World Cup, the world's most-watched sporting event. During the tournament, South African fans blew on loud horns called *vuvuzelas*, an essential part of being a soccer fan in South Africa. Five soccer stadiums were built for the tournament, and five more were refurbished to host the games. Nine South African cities played host to the matches. In the six years it took to prepare for the event, the South African government spent billions of dollars on construction, security, and transportation. Hosting the games gave the country's economy a boost, trained workers with lasting skills, increased tourism, and improved the nation's infrastructure.

South Africa also has indigenous sports, which children grow up playing together in their neighborhoods and at school. Among these sports are *kgati*, a rope-skipping game, and *dibeke*, a ball game similar to kickball.

FILM, LITERATURE, AND TELEVISION

South Africa has a small film industry. In recent years, the government has supported the industry in hopes of making South Africa a destination for foreign filmmakers and increasing the number of locally produced films. Still, many directors and actors go abroad to find success. Academy Award winner Charlize Theron is South Africa's best-known actress.

South Africa is home to many famous authors. During the apartheid era, books dealing with the country's politics were commonly banned within South Africa. This had the effect of driving many writers out of the country. One of South Africa's most famous novelists is Alan Paton, author of *Cry, the Beloved Country*. Two South Africans have been awarded the Nobel Prize in Literature: J. M. Coetzee won in 2003 and Nadine Gordimer won in 1991. In 1946, Peter Abrahams wrote the first novel to explore the dehumanizing effects of racism. Other South African authors who used their pens to fight apartheid include

Charlize Theron was the first South African woman to win an Oscar.

South African actress Charlize Theron has found international success.

NOBEL PEACE PRIZE WINNERS

South Africa claims four Nobel Peace Prize winners among its citizens: African National Congress President Albert Luthuli, Archbishop Desmond Tutu, and former South African Presidents F. W. de Klerk and Nelson Mandela.

Luthuli was a teacher, Christian lay minister, tribal chief, and human rights activist in the 1950s and 1960s. He was awarded the Nobel Peace Prize in 1960. Archbishop Desmond Tutu received the Nobel Peace Prize in 1984 for trying to make peace between the ruling Nationalist Party and the black resistance groups.

F. W. de Klerk, president from 1989 to 1994, left no doubt that apartheid would come to an end under his leadership. De Klerk shared the 1993 Nobel Peace Prize with Nelson Mandela, whom he had released from prison in 1990. During Mandela's 27 years behind bars, he was offered conditional release but refused to compromise his principles. Mandela served as South Africa's president from 1994 to 1999.

playwright Athol Fugard, novelist Es'kia Mphahlele, and playwright and novelist Zakes Mda.

Television did not come to South Africa until 1976, nearly 60 years after its introduction in the United States. Programming was strictly controlled by the government, and it avoided discussion of politics. News coverage of the resistance movement was not allowed. Today, South Africa has a free, independent, and diverse media, as guaranteed by South Africa's constitution. South Africa has 21 daily newspapers, 92 television stations, and 137 radio stations.[1]

ARCHITECTURE

South African architecture incorporates styles from every corner of the world. There are mud huts, stone castles, monuments to the Boer founders, township shacks, suburban mansions, mosques, cathedrals, safari camps, and high-rise luxury hotels.

Rondavels, which are circular homes with thatched roofs, are found all over South Africa. Traditionally, the floors and walls are made of stones, mud, or cow dung. These structures have become popular as overnight huts for tourists and visitors to the game reserves.

Immigrants to South Africa brought their own styles of building. The Dutch influence is seen in Cape Town and nearby, where the Cape Dutch architecture, with its whitewashed walls and curved gables, is common. The Western Cape towns of Stellenbosch and Franschhoek are known for their beautiful examples of this building style.

South Africa has the longest railroad network in sub-Saharan Africa.

During the period of British rule, government buildings, universities, and churches in South Africa were constructed in typical imperial style, with columns and stairs leading up to massive stone buildings. The old House of Parliament in Cape Town and Durban's city hall are examples of this British influence on South Africa's architecture.

Traditional rondavels, Coffee Bay, South Africa

Modern building projects in South Africa are changing the skylines of its cities. The largest project was to build five new soccer stadiums for the 2010 FIFA (Fédération Internationale de Football Association) World Cup. In 2003, a new cable bridge named for Nelson Mandela opened in Johannesburg.

CULTURAL VILLAGES

Tribal life continues for some South Africans, such as the Shangaans in Mpumalanga Province. They create artwork for sale and also invite visitors to come and see what life is like in a traditional African village. Tourists can pay to have a guided tour of the village, share a meal with the tribe, and see the tribe members perform in a festival. Lesedi, Matsamo, and Khaya La Bantu are other cultural villages in South Africa. Visitors to these villages gain some insights into tribal culture and provide the tribes with a source of income and a way to preserve their traditions.

CHAPTER 7
POLITICS: A NEW DEMOCRACY

Today, South Africa is a multiracial democracy. Since the end of apartheid in 1994, four national elections have been held. Observers inside and outside the country have declared the balloting to be free and fair. People of all races now vote for leaders to represent them. These leaders work together across the various levels of government—local, provincial, and national—to uphold the constitution. While South Africa still faces problems, its transition from a minority white-ruled state to a multiracial democracy is considered one of the great success stories of the twentieth century.

South Africa has a multiparty political system. In the national election in 2009, 26 political parties participated and 77 percent of the citizens registered to vote—a total of 17.6 million people—cast ballots.[1] While many parties participate in the political process, the ANC, which

South Africans stand in long lines waiting to exercise their right to vote.

"We have confronted and successfully dealt with some of the toughest, most intractable challenges of our time—challenges that have left other societies in ashes. We are problem solvers. We are pragmatists. We work by consensus. And we prefer long-term solutions to quick, expedient fixes. But we are still revolutionaries: we want to hand succeeding generations a truly better world."[4]

—Barbara Masekela, South African ambassador to the United States (2003–)

played a leading role in representing the interests of the black majority under apartheid, continues to dominate. Every South African president elected since 1994 has been an ANC member.

A NEW CONSTITUTION

After the legalization of the ANC and the release and return of many political prisoners, the old white leadership and the new black leadership began working together to create an interim constitution that would serve as the supreme law of the nation. This document went into effect in 1993 and remained the nation's law until it was replaced on February 4, 1997, by the new Constitution of the Republic of South Africa.[2] This constitution is considered one of the most progressive in the world, prohibiting discrimination on the basis of race, gender, pregnancy, marital status, color, sexual orientation, age, disability, religion, conscience, belief, culture, language, birth, and ethnic or social origin.[3]

In addition, the constitution established the one-person, one-vote law, giving all citizens over age 18 a voice in the country's government. Other important aspects of the constitution establish the freedoms of expression and assembly, the rights to life and to human dignity, and the right of citizens to live where they want and come and go as they choose. South Africa's constitution determined that the new nation would have eleven official languages, nine provinces, and three capitals. It also established a parliamentary system of government with proportional representation, in which a party's seats in parliament are designated according to the number of votes cast. The party with the most members controls legislating, but minority opinions are also represented. The elected members of parliament choose a leader, who acts as the nation's president.

"We, the people of South Africa,
Recognize the injustices of our past;
Honor those who suffered for justice and freedom in our land;
    Respect those who have worked to build and develop our country; and Believe that South Africa belongs to all who live in it, united in our diversity. We therefore, through our freely elected representatives, adopt this Constitution."[5]

—From the preamble to South Africa's constitution, 1996

The National Assembly Chamber in Cape Town

SYSTEM OF GOVERNMENT

There are three levels of government in South Africa—national, provincial, and local—and elections are held for offices at each level. At the national level, there are three branches of government: legislative, executive, and judicial. At the provincial level, each of the nine provinces has its own legislature, charged with making laws. At the local level, South Africa has 283 municipalities governed by municipal councils, which implement local laws and oversee local government.[6]

At the national level, South Africa's legislative branch, or parliament, is comprised of two houses: the National Assembly and the National Council of Provinces. The National Assembly has between 350 and

STRUCTURE OF THE GOVERNMENT OF SOUTH AFRICA

Constitution		
Legislature (Parliament)	Executive	Judiciary (Court System)
National Assembly National Council of Provinces	President Deputy President Cabinet Ministers	Constitutional Court Supreme Court of Appeal High Courts Magistrates Courts

400 members who are elected by the people from their districts for a five-year term. The National Council of Provinces has 90 members, ten delegates from each province, who represent the interests of the provinces at the national level. Both houses of parliament are based in Cape Town.

The executive branch of government at the national level is comprised of the president, a deputy president, and a group of cabinet ministers. The president's job as head of state is to "uphold, defend and respect the Constitution as the supreme law of the Republic."[7] The president is not a member of parliament, but he or she is elected by the National Assembly at its first meeting after a general election. The president then selects a deputy president and cabinet ministers from the National Assembly. Presidents serve a term of five years and may be reelected once to serve a second term. Pretoria, the former national capital, continues to be the government's administrative capital.

South Africa was called the Union of South Africa from 1910 until 1961.

The third branch of government in South Africa is the judiciary. The judicial system comprises the courts, which are independent from the other branches of government. The role of the courts is to uphold the nation's constitution and laws. Judiciary bodies, from the highest to the lowest level of authority, include the Constitutional Court, the Supreme Court of Appeal, the High Courts, and the Magistrates Courts. The Constitutional Court is in Johannesburg, and the Supreme Court is located in Bloemfontein.

South Africa's executive branch meets in the Union Buildings in Pretoria.

SOUTH AFRICA'S FLAG AND ITS SYMBOLISM

The new flag of South Africa was created to symbolize the unity of the people and the new democratic nation. First used in 1994, it is the world's only six-colored flag. The colors that appear in the flag—green, black, yellow, red, white, and blue—have been historically important to the diverse people of South Africa and contain different symbolism for different people, according to the government of South Africa. The horizontal Y symbolizes South Africa's diverse peoples joining together to become one.

Fourteen High Courts are located around the country in various divisions. There are several hundred Magistrates Courts around the nation.

In addition, other government agencies oversee or represent various aspects of South African life. Under the constitution, a Public Protector's office was established to act as an advocate for private citizens involved in disputes with governmental entities. A Human Rights Commission was established, as well, to monitor and ensure that the rights of citizens are respected.

Traditional leaders also play a role in public life in South Africa. They are given representation in the National House of Traditional Leaders and also at the provincial level in several provinces that have large populations of citizens practicing traditional cultures.

Flag of South Africa

MAJOR POLITICAL PARTIES

In South Africa's first democratic election, held in 1994, the ANC won 252 seats, totaling 62.6 percent of the vote. In the second election, in 1999, the ANC won 266 seats, or 66.4 percent of the vote. In the 2004 election, the ANC gained even more power, with 279 seats, totaling 69.7 percent of the vote. The ANC continues to be the leading political party in South Africa. In the 2009 election, it won 65.9 percent of the vote, earning 264 seats.[8]

Other parties that continue to play a minority role in South African politics are the Zulu-based Inkatha Freedom Party and some newly emerging parties, such as the Congress of the People and the Democratic Alliance. Inkatha, which is led by Zulu chief Mangosuthu Buthelezi, receives support mostly from the Zulu people, who are concentrated in KwaZulu-Natal Province. Buthelezi has led the party since 1975. The Democratic Alliance, led by Helen Zille, is the largest opposition party. It advocates free market policies, individual freedoms, and limitations on government. The new Congress of the People was formed by dissatisfied members of the ANC. It is a progressive democratic party aimed at promoting social justice and human rights. It posted its first slate of candidates in the 2009 elections.

Since South African blacks have had the right to vote, they have turned out to exercise this privilege in great numbers, giving the nation an overall voting rate

South Africans own more than 46 million cell phones, nearly one for each of its 49 million people.

South African voters rally in support of their political party.

President Jacob Zuma, *center*, faced corruption charges prior to his presidency, but the charges were withdrawn.

much higher than the rates of most developed countries. In 1999, of the 18.1 million registered voters in South Africa, approximately 15.9 million cast ballots, representing 87.9 percent participation in the election. There was a similarly high turnout in 2004, with 76.7 percent of registered voters casting ballots. In 2009, 77 percent of the nation's 23.1 million registered voters cast ballots.[9]

CURRENT LEADERS

The men who have served as president of South Africa since 1999, when Nelson Mandela finished his term, have found it difficult to follow in Mandela's footsteps. Thabo Mbeki was elected in 1999, but he resigned in 2008. He was in the midst of a power struggle with one-time deputy party leader Jacob Zuma. Kgalema Motlanthe served out the final seven months of Mbeki's presidential term after his resignation. Zuma became president of South Africa in 2009. An ANC member, like his predecessors, he was also a political prisoner on Robben Island and then, following his release, an exiled leader of the struggle against apartheid.

AFRIKANER DISCONTENT

Since the end of apartheid and the establishment of democracy in South Africa, some Afrikaners have advocated for their own independent homeland, which they call a *volkstaat*, or "people's state." They have proposed creating this land in Northern Cape Province. The Freedom Front Plus, a political party that represents Afrikaner interests, received less than 1 percent of votes in recent elections.[10]

CHAPTER 8

ECONOMICS: THE BOUNTY OF THE LAND

South Africa's economy has always been linked to its land and natural resources. Since Cape Colony's founding in 1652, its strategic location made it a stopping-off point where ships could be loaded with fresh fruits, vegetables, and meat. Two centuries later, people came to stake a claim in the region's gold and diamond mines. Even today, South Africa's major exports are mining and agricultural products. But the economy has expanded to include small businesses, transportation, manufacturing, and tourism.

MINING AND INDUSTRY

In addition to gold and diamonds, South Africans mine other natural resources including platinum, chromium, antimony, zirconium, titanium,

Ranchers raise sheep on the Highveld. Ranching is one of the many agricultural businesses that thrive in South Africa.

CURRENCY

South Africa's currency is the rand, which was originally introduced when the Republic of South Africa was established in 1961. One hundred cents makes up one rand. Paper notes come in denominations of 10, 20, 50, 100, and 200 rand, and the animals of South Africa are represented on them. Coins come in denominations of 1 cent, 2 cents, 5 cents, 10 cents, 20 cents, 50 cents, 1 rand, 2 rand, and 5 rand. The symbol for the rand is R. In 2011, one South African rand was worth about 14 US cents, or US$1= R6.93.

iron ore, nickel, phosphates, tin, copper, uranium, coal, vermiculite, and manganese. According to some reports, South Africa is the world's largest producer of platinum, manganese, chromium, and vanadium. It is also the second-largest producer of gold, zirconium, and titanium and the fourth-largest producer of diamonds.[1]

South Africa's mining legacy was one of exploiting its poor black workers. The best jobs were reserved for whites. Blacks had to work long hours in dangerous conditions and live away from their families in dormitory-style housing near the mines. Safety conditions have improved over the years, however. Unions were set up to ensure that workers receive adequate pay and housing. Today, many of the mine workers in South Africa come from neighboring countries.

In the future, more previously disadvantaged blacks will be able to share in the financial rewards of their country's mineral wealth. Government legislation has been created that will require mining

South African miners heading to work

BLACK ECONOMIC EMPOWERMENT

The South African government has created policies to offer benefits and incentives to companies owned or managed by blacks. The system is called Black Economic Empowerment, or BEE. The goal is to aid black people, who were disadvantaged for so long, by helping them get started in the business world. The policy has proven controversial, however, with critics calling it reverse discrimination against white-owned businesses and white workers.

companies to employ more black workers in managerial positions. In addition, a new government target calls for 51 percent of future mining projects to be controlled by black-owned companies.[2]

South Africa makes many products—some for its own market and others for export to other countries. Among the items manufactured are autos, textiles, chemicals, iron, steel, and machinery. South Africa's major trading partners are China, the United States, Japan, Germany, and the United Kingdom.

AGRICULTURE

South Africa grows enough food to feed its people plus more. Corn, wheat, fruit, and sugarcane are the nation's major crops. South Africa also exports agricultural goods, including grain, meat, fruits, and vegetables. The country has a competitive advantage by having seasons that run opposite those in Europe, which means it can export summer fruits and vegetables when they are not locally available during winter in the Northern Hemisphere.

Resources of South Africa

Only 13 percent of the land in South Africa can support agriculture, due to inadequate water supplies.[3] Even so, the country has both large-scale commercial agriculture, mostly run by whites, and small farms and ranches, mostly operated by black farmers. The best agricultural land has long been under white control. Since the end of apartheid, there has been an effort to redistribute farmland in a more equitable way.

ROOIBOS TEA

Rooibos is an Afrikaans word meaning "red bush." It describes the native South African bush that is used to produce a tea that has recently become popular in Europe and the United States. This herbal tea has long been enjoyed in South Africa. It has been found to be rich in antioxidants, which have many health benefits. The rooibos bush is grown only in the Western Cape and has become a major export of the area.

One of South Africa's must successful agricultural exports is wine. The country ranks ninth in the world in total wine production.[4] Wineries in the Western Cape region produce wines that are regarded as among the world's best.

TOURISM

South Africa's new era of democracy opened the door not only to investment by international business but also to tourists who had long avoided the country. Approximately 9 million foreigners visited in 2007. Tourism has become a major growth industry, employing 7 percent of South Africans.[5]

People come to South Africa to conduct business and to see wildlife, watch and play sports, and enjoy the country's beaches and warm weather. Because of South Africa's advanced medical system, relatively low costs, and highly trained doctors, it is also a prime destination for people seeking medical treatments.

Many tourists come to South Africa to see majestic animals such as lions.

ENERGY

Most of South Africa's energy needs are filled by locally mined coal. Eskom, a state-owned energy company, generates 95 percent of the electricity used in South Africa and 45 percent of the electricity used on the continent of Africa. Coal is used to run power stations and produces much of the nation's electricity. Some coal is also converted into liquid fuel. Nuclear power provides 6 percent of the nation's electricity.[6] According to a 2009 estimate, South Africa produces 192,000 barrels of oil per day, but it consumed 532,000 barrels per day, meaning it had to import oil to meet its needs.[7]

Future plans call for building more nuclear power plants, generating power from the wind, and harnessing the sun to produce solar power. In 2010, 20 percent of South African homes did not have electricity.[8] Most of these homes are in townships and rural areas.

CHRISTIAAN BARNARD

The world's first successful human heart transplant was performed in Cape Town in 1967 by Dr. Christiaan Barnard. Although the patient survived only 18 days, this pioneering surgery was a major medical breakthrough. Over the years, Barnard and other cardiac surgeons improved their methods, and today, a patient can live for many years with a transplanted heart.

INFRASTRUCTURE

South Africa is considered an emerging market, which means it is not a first-world developed nation like the United States, Japan, and the countries of Europe. But South Africa is the most advanced country in Africa. It has its own stock exchange and well-developed infrastructure.

South Africa has an excellent transportation network, including roads, railways, marine terminals and ports, buses, and airports that connect both small and large cities. Public transportation is available and affordable in the cities, but getting around rural areas can be a challenge without a private vehicle. Between 2005 and 2010, while preparations were underway for hosting the 2010 FIFA World Cup, the government invested billions of dollars to upgrade its transportation network.

Communication in South Africa is improving, although many people are still without modern communications. In 2008, an estimated 34.1 million mobile phones were in use in the country. Five million people, or 10 percent of the population, had Internet

SOLAR POWER

Northern Cape Province is a prime location for a solar energy–generating plant, because it gets abundant sunshine nearly year-round. Plans are underway to build a massive solar park in this largely uninhabited, semidesert region. The South African government is developing the project with the help of the Clinton Climate Change Initiative. The project will cost an estimated 150 billion rand (approximately US$20.5 billion) and could begin delivering electricity as early as 2012.[9]

access.[10] In rural and isolated areas, where Internet access is mostly unavailable, local post offices provide limited access for free.

ECONOMIC CHALLENGES

Before 1994, South African blacks had few economic or educational opportunities, and most lived in poverty. The best jobs were reserved for whites. The new democratic government created policies aimed at helping blacks get the education and job training they needed for careers that would bring them decent wages. But unemployment, which was 23.3 percent in 2010, remains a major problem.[11]

South Africa has the second-least equal distribution of wealth in the world.

The gross domestic product (GDP) per capita in 2010 was estimated at $10,700, but this does not tell the real story about how people live.[12] Approximately half of all South Africans live in poverty, while the other half live in relative comfort. As recently as 2006, government studies found that wealth was unequally distributed by race—48.2 percent of all wealth was earned by whites, even though that group represents only approximately 9 or 10 percent of the total population. Blacks, who make up almost 80 percent of the population, take home 38.8 percent of the wealth.[13]

The South African rand features animals including leopards, rhinoceroses, elephants, and Cape buffalo.

CHAPTER 9
SOUTH AFRICA TODAY

South Africa reinvented itself in the twentieth century. Citizens stood up against their government's racist policies, creating a resistance movement that brought worldwide attention and support and led to international isolation of the apartheid regime. Decades of racist policies, which made the majority of the nation's population second-class citizens, ultimately failed. And by the end of the century, a black president, Nelson Mandela, ushered in a new era of democracy.

The world rejoiced with South Africa's rebirth. But the reality quickly sunk in that the inequalities that had been institutionalized for generations could not be fixed overnight. Allowing citizens of all races to participate in selecting their government did not solve the problems of poverty. Neither did putting in place a new constitution.

South Africa has won 19 medals at the Summer Olympics since 1992.

Spectators wave South African flags at the 2010 World Cup. The successful event has given the country hope for its future progress.

UBUNTU

South Africans have a philosophy of *ubuntu*, a Xhosa and Zulu word that translates into "I am because we are." *Ubuntu* expresses the long-held African philosophy that all people share a common humanity and that one person's actions can affect the prosperity of all. *Ubuntu* was established as a founding principle of the new democracy.

Nelson Mandela was a unifying force. He had the respect of the vast majority of South Africans—blacks, whites, and everyone in between. But after his five years as president ended in 1999, criticism of the slow pace of change grew stronger. People wondered when they would get decent jobs, good schools, safe neighborhoods, better health care, and homes to call their own.

Many black homes in South Africa have many generations living under one roof. It is not unusual for an extended family—including aunts, uncles, and cousins—to live in one home, sharing resources and child-care duties. This situation is often due to poverty, but it is also a tradition among blacks, who generally have strong ties to family. Parents commonly spend hours commuting to and from jobs far away from home, while the grandparents take care of the children.

Despite cramped living conditions, many extended families live together under one roof.

EDUCATION AND UNEMPLOYMENT

Almost as many girls as boys attend school in South Africa. Depending on where they live, they may or may not have friends of different races and ethnicities. Many wealthy families still pay to send their children to expensive private schools, which are often nearly all white. Poorer areas, which have state-funded schools, are usually all black. Many are crowded, and some have no playing field or running water. In the cities and middle-class suburbs, much more mixing of the races has occurred. Students wear school uniforms at almost all schools, public and private. A new generation of affordable private schools is cropping up, giving some poor children a chance at a better education.

Teenagers in South Africa are required to attend school through at least the ninth grade or age 15. This is better than what is required in most African countries, but many children do not continue with school and then have trouble finding a job. Often, this leads to a life of crime, violence, or other problems. Teenage pregnancy, a high rate of HIV/AIDS infection, and unemployment are major problems facing young people in South Africa, especially those with a lower level of education. The nation's many AIDS orphans are especially vulnerable.

Poverty and lack of education are closely linked. Under apartheid, educating blacks and mixed-race people was not considered important because they were destined for menial jobs. This legacy has caused continuing

Life expectancy in South Africa decreased by ten years between 1997 and 2007.

Progressive Primary School in Johannesburg gives poor South Africans the opportunity for a better education.

poverty and unemployment among poorly educated blacks and mixed-race people. Former president F. W. de Klerk began the integration of schools, which had been separated by race. Black schools had historically been overcrowded and underfunded, while white schools had smaller classes, better-trained teachers, and modern equipment.

MILLENNIUM DEVELOPMENT GOALS

At the United Nations Millennium Summit in 2000, 189 countries, including South Africa, signed a declaration of eight critical economic and social development priorities. Their goal is to achieve the following by 2015:

"1. Eradicate extreme poverty and hunger

2. Achieve universal primary education

3. Promote gender equality and empower women

4. Reduce child mortality

5. Improve maternal health

6. Combat HIV/AIDS, malaria and other diseases

7. Environmental sustainability

8. Global partnership"[2]

Children who have grown up since apartheid ended, known as "born frees," have benefited from the nation's new education policies.[1] However, there is a lost generation of people who missed out on an education and are stuck in low-paying, unskilled jobs with little prospect of improvement. A major effort has been made to educate these people and to teach them job skills. Literacy leapt from 76.2 percent in 1990 to 84.8 percent in 2000, and steady gains have continued through the first decade of the twenty-first century.

The literacy rate stood at 89.3 percent in 2010.[3] Even so, as of 2007, only 18.6 percent of South Africans had completed a secondary education, and only 9.1 percent went on to higher education.[4]

A significant achievement is that South Africa now provides nearly universal access to primary education. With almost one-third of all South Africans under the age of 15, these efforts will pay off with a better-educated workforce, as today's schoolchildren grow into adulthood.

A NEW MIDDLE CLASS

Even though the majority of black South Africans are still poor, there is a fast-growing black middle class. A 2007 study found that membership in this group increased by 30 percent over a 15-month period.[5] With their increased spending power, these people are leaving the townships and moving into traditionally white suburbs and schools, seeking a better future for their families.

HEALTH

One of the greatest challenges facing South Africa is unequal access to health care and medicine. Many people either cannot afford to see a doctor or have to wait a long time for an appointment. The government has created public clinics for those who cannot pay for medical care, and more doctors and nurses are being trained to meet the growing need for these professionals. Yet despite these improvements, both the death rate for children under age five and the maternal death rate have risen in the past decade.

The greatest health crisis in South Africa comes from HIV/AIDS, which prevents a person's immune system from functioning properly. In 2009, an estimated 5.6 million South Africans were living with HIV/AIDS, the highest number of any country.[6] This high rate of infection has reduced the life expectancy in South Africa, which is now approximately 50 years.[7] By comparison, the average life expectancy in most European countries, the United States, and Canada is approximately 80 years.

HOUSING AND LAND

When the new democratic era began in 1994, South Africa had a severe shortage of adequate housing for its poorest people. Many homes in the black townships lacked running water, electricity, and toilets, creating conditions that often led to health problems for the people living in these dirty and crowded areas. As of 2007, an estimated 80 percent of South Africans had electricity, 88.6 percent had running water, and 60.4 percent had flush toilets.[8] The South African government has made a major effort to house the nation's people, and by 2009, it had built 2.8 million homes, giving shelter to 13.5 million people at no charge.[9] The government's goal is to have all citizens in adequate housing by 2014.

One of the most difficult challenges faced by South Africa's government is land redistribution. During the apartheid era and earlier, blacks were robbed of what was previously theirs. For example, the best farmland was taken away and given to white farmers. Similarly, blacks and mixed-race people were told to leave the nicest neighborhoods in the cities. Their houses were torn down, and white families were allowed

A South African choir sings to raise awareness of HIV/AIDS on World AIDS Day, December 1, 2008.

to build homes in their place. Making up for the wrongs of the past is not easy. Is it fair to tell a white farmer to leave the land his family has worked for generations? How can one family be compensated for their loss without unfairly hurting another family? These are tricky questions, and finding solutions is not easy or quick.

LOOKING TO THE FUTURE

South Africa has come a long way in a short time. It chose peaceful negotiation over a bloody revolution. It created a constitution admired by the world. It has made real progress in bringing about an equitable multiracial society. Some citizens have seen their lives improve dramatically. People who could not read in the past are now in school and on track for starting careers. People who lived in tin shacks now own well-built homes and the proper facilities in which to raise a family. The country still faces many challenges, but for many South Africans, the future looks much brighter than the past.

"The fact that South Africa is in many respects the admiration of the world is not a matter of accident. It is a result of the hard work of men and women who sacrificed so our country could join humanity in the search for a better world. And with such a leadership, with such organized formations determined to build partnerships for change, what more can we say, but that there is hope for South Africa! All we need to do together is to turn this hope into reality."

—*President Nelson Mandela, State of the Nation Address, February 10, 1999*[10]

With energy and enthusiasm, the people of South Africa are improving their economy while preserving their cultural heritage.

TIMELINE

3 million years ago	Early human ancestors live in the area of South Africa.
ca. 300 CE	Bantu-speaking people arrive in South Africa.
1488	Portuguese explorer Bartholomeu Dias becomes the first European to round the tip of Africa.
1806	The British win control of Cape Colony from the Dutch.
1816–1828	Shaka rules the Zulu.
1834	The British abolish slavery in Cape Colony, angering the Boers.
1838	The Boers kill an estimated 3,000 Zulu warriors at the Battle of Blood River.
1867	Diamonds are discovered near Kimberley, attracting many immigrants who seek to stake a claim.
1899–1902	The British and the Boers fight the Anglo-Boer War.
1910	The Union of South Africa is created, uniting the former Boer republics with the British Natal and Cape Provinces. Britain approves the South Africa Act, reserving the right to vote for whites only.
1912	The South African Native National Congress is founded; it later becomes the African National Congress (ANC).
1913	The Natives' Land Act prohibits blacks from buying land anywhere except those areas specifically set aside for them in reserves.

1948	The Afrikaner-led National Party wins the election and begins implementing the policy of apartheid.
1952	Blacks are required to carry passes and not allowed in white areas.
1955	Resistance leaders write the Freedom Charter, pledging to work together to gain the freedoms that have been taken away from them and to create a democratic South Africa.
1960	At Sharpeville, police kill 69 unarmed protesters and injure hundreds more during a march against the pass laws.
1961	South Africa becomes an independent republic and leaves the British Commonwealth.
1962	Nelson Mandela and other ANC leaders are arrested and soon found guilty of sabotage. They are eventually sentenced to life in prison.
1976	Soweto police kill 600 protesters demonstrating against the use of Afrikaans in schools.
1990	New South African President F. W. de Klerk lifts the ban on the ANC and releases Nelson Mandela and other political prisoners from jail.
1994	South Africa holds its first multiracial free and fair election. Nelson Mandela becomes president, after the ANC wins nearly two-thirds of the votes.
1999	Thabo Mbeki is elected president.
2008	Mbeki resigns under pressure from ANC party leadership.
2009	Jacob Zuma is elected president.

FACTS AT YOUR FINGERTIPS

GEOGRAPHY

Official name: Republic of South Africa

Area: 470,693 square miles (1,219,090 sq km)

Climate: Much of the country is mild and dry, similar to California, or mild and humid, similar to the coast of the Gulf of Mexico.

Highest elevation: Njesuthi mountain, 11,181 feet (3,408 m) above sea level

Lowest elevation: Atlantic Ocean, 0 feet (0 m) above sea level

Significant geographic features: Cape Agulhas, the southernmost tip of Africa

PEOPLE

Population (July 2011 est.): 49,004,031

Most populous city: Johannesburg

Ethnic groups: Blacks (Bantu origin), 79.4 percent; Whites (European origin), 9.2 percent; Coloured, 8.8 percent; Indian/Asian, 2.6 percent

Percentage of residents living in urban areas: 61 percent

Life expectancy: 49.2 years at birth (world ranking 215th)

Language(s): 11 official languages; English, isiZulu, isiXhosa, isiNdebele, Afrikaans, isiSwati, Sesotho, Sepedi, Setswana, Tshivenda, and Xitsonga

Religion(s): Christian, 80 percent; Islamic, 1.5 percent; Hindu, 1.2 percent; Jewish, African traditionalist, or other, less than 1 percent; no religious beliefs, 15 percent

GOVERNMENT AND ECONOMY

Government: republic

Capitals: South Africa has three capitals:

- Cape Town hosts the two legislative bodies which make up the parliament: the National Assembly and the National Council of Provinces.

- Pretoria hosts the executive branch of government.

- Bloemfontein hosts the judicial branch.

Date of adoption of current constitution: December 10, 1996

Head of government and state: president, legislature

Currency: rand

Industries and natural resources: mining, especially platinum, gold, and chromium; manufacturing, including machinery, textiles, chemicals, and iron and steel; agriculture, including cereal crops, livestock, wine, and fruit and vegetables

NATIONAL SYMBOLS

Holidays:

- New Year's Day, January 1
- Human Rights Day, March 21
- Family Day, Monday after Easter
- Freedom Day, April 27
- Workers Day, May 1
- Youth Day, June 16
- Women's Day, August 9
- Heritage Day, September 24
- Reconciliation Day, December 16
- Christmas Day, December 25
- Day of Goodwill, December 26

Flag: Includes six colors: green, black, yellow, red, white, and blue. It features a horizontal Y, which symbolizes diversity becoming unity.

National anthem: A combined version of "Nkosi Sikelel' iAfrika" ("God Bless Africa") and "The Call of South Africa" ("Die Stem"), adopted in 1994.

National fish: Galjoen

National bird: Blue crane

National animal: Springbok

National flower: King Protea

National tree: Real yellowwood

KEY PEOPLE

F. W. de Klerk, credited with helping end apartheid and usher in a democratic era in South Africa. He shared the Nobel Peace Prize with Nelson Mandela in 1993.

Nelson Rolihlahla Mandela led the resistance movement against apartheid until he was jailed as a political prisoner for 27 years. He was elected South Africa's first black president in the nation's first democratic election, held in 1994.

Archbishop Desmond Tutu was awarded the Nobel Peace Prize in 1984 for his leadership in fighting the racist policies of the South African government.

PROVINCES OF SOUTH AFRICA

Province; Capital

Eastern Cape; Bisho

Free State; Bloemfontein

Gauteng; Johannesburg

KwaZulu-Natal; Pietermaritzburg

Limpopo; Polokwane

Mpumalanga; Nelspruit

North West; Mafikeng

Northern Cape; Kimberley

Western Cape; Cape Town

GLOSSARY

Afrikaner

A member of the ethnic group composed mainly of Afrikaans-speaking South Africans of European descent (mainly Dutch, German, and French).

apartheid

A social policy of racial segregation involving political, economic, and legal discrimination against people who are not white.

Bantu

A member of one of the many linguistically related peoples of central and southern Africa.

biodiversity

The variety of plant and animal life found in a particular habitat.

Boer

A colonist or farmer in South Africa, usually of Dutch descent.

coloured

A South African person of mixed race.

gross domestic product

A measure of a country's economy; the total of all goods and services produced in a country in a year.

indigenous

Originally or naturally belonging to an area.

reconciliation

The reestablishing of friendly relations or compatibility.

sanctions

Punishing measures adopted by one country or a group of countries against another country for political reasons.

township

In South Africa, an area set aside for black occupation.

treason

The crime of betraying one's government.

ADDITIONAL RESOURCES

SELECTED BIBLIOGRAPHY

De Villiers, Melissa, et al. *Insight Guides South Africa.* Singapore: APA, 2004. Print.

Diagram Group, The. *Peoples of Southern Africa.* New York: Facts on File, 1997. Print.

Thompson, Leonard. *A History of South Africa.* New Haven, CT: Yale Nota Bene, 2001. Print.

FURTHER READINGS

Carlin, John. *Playing the Enemy: Nelson Mandela and the Game That Made a Nation.* New York: Penguin, 2008. Print.

Keller, Bill. *Tree Shaker: The Story of Nelson Mandela.* Boston: Kingfisher, 2008. Print.

Lans, Hans. *The Story of My Life: South Africa Seen through the Eyes of Its Children.* Cape Town: Kwela Books, 2002. Print.

Paton, Alan. *Cry, the Beloved Country.* New York: Scribner, 2003. Print.

WEB LINKS

To learn more about South Africa, visit ABDO Publishing Company online at **www.abdopublishing.com**. Web sites about South Africa are featured on our Book Links page. These links are routinely monitored and updated to provide the most current information available.

PLACES TO VISIT

If you are ever in South Africa, consider checking out these important and interesting sites!

The Cradle of Humankind World Heritage Site

Located in Gauteng Province, the Cradle of Humankind includes a museum and visitor's center that teaches about the evolutionary history of humans. Visitors can enter the caves where ancient fossils were discovered.

Kruger National Park

Located in Mpumalanga and Limpopo Provinces, Kruger National Park protects animals, habitats, and archaeological sites ranging from early humans to nineteenth-century European settlers.

Robben Island Prison Museum

Located off the coast of Cape Town, Robben Island once held political prisoners including Nelson Mandela. Today, the former prison is a museum and a UNESCO World Heritage site.

SOURCE NOTES

CHAPTER 1. A VISIT TO SOUTH AFRICA

1. Nelson Mandela. "Speech at Freedom Day Celebrations, April 27, 1999." *South African Government Information.* Government Communications and Information System [South Africa], 27 Apr. 1999. Web. 27 Oct. 2010.

CHAPTER 2. GEOGRAPHY: NATURAL WONDERS

1. "South Africa." *Encyclopædia Britannica.* Encyclopædia Britannica, 2011. Web. 14 Jan. 2011.

2. "Vredefort Dome." *World Heritage Convention.* UNESCO World Heritage Centre, 2011. Web. 26 Jan. 2011.

3. "The World Factbook: South Africa." *Central Intelligence Agency.* Central Intelligence Agency, 20 Jan. 2011. Web. 26 Jan. 2011.

4. "Monthly Averages." *Weather Channel.* Weather Channel, n.d. Web. 9 May 2011.

5. "South Africa." *Encyclopædia Britannica.* Encyclopædia Britannica, 2011. Web. 14 Jan. 2011.

6. "Orange River." *Encyclopædia Britannica.* Encyclopædia Britannica, 2011. Web. 14 Jan. 2011.

CHAPTER 3. ANIMALS AND NATURE: A LAND OF BIODIVERSITY

1. "Environment." *South African Government Information.* Government Communications and Information System [South Africa], 5 July 2010. Web. 27 Oct. 2010.

2. "Cape Floral Region Protected Areas." *World Heritage Convention.* UNESCO World Heritage Centre, 2011. Web. 26 Jan. 2011.

3. "Kruger National Park." *South African National Parks.* South African National Parks, 2010. Web. 22 Jan. 2011.

4. Michelle Faul. "Tourists Pay Top Dollar to Shoot Captive Lions." *San Diego Union-Tribune.* 15 Oct. 2010. Print. A-7.

5. Ibid.

6. Ibid.

7. "White Paper on the Conservation and Sustainable Use of South Africa's Biological Diversity. Chapter 1: Introduction." *South African Government Information.* Government Communications and Information System [South Africa], 1997. Web. 22 Jan. 2011.

8. "Summary Statistics: Summaries by Country, Table 5, Threatened Species in Each Country." *IUCN Red List of Threatened Species.* International Union for Conservation of Nature and Natural Resources, 2010. Web. 18 Jan. 2011.

9. "2010 Worst Year for Rhino Poaching." *South African National Parks.* South African National Parks, 11 Jan. 2011. Web. 22 Jan. 2011.

CHAPTER 4. HISTORY: A COMPLICATED PAST

1. "Intervention from Above: The 1913 Natives' Land Act." *South African History Online.* South African History Online, n.d. Web. 27 Oct. 2010.

2. "Freedom Charter and the Congress of the People. 26 June 1955. *South African History Online.* South African History Online, n.d. Web. 22 Jan. 2011.

3. Nelson Mandela. "Address to Rally in Cape Town on His Release from Prison, Feb. 11, 1990." *South African Government Information.* Government Communications and Information System [South Africa], 11 Feb. 1990. Web. 28 Oct. 2010.

4. "African National Congress." *Encyclopædia Britannica.* Encyclopædia Britannica, 2011. Web. 14 Feb. 2011.

5. Christie Ritter. "More Than 1,000 Vote in San Diego." *San Diego Union-Tribune.* 27 April 1994. Print.

6. Ibid.

7. "National and Provincial Elections Results." *Independent Electoral Commission South Africa.* IEC, 2011. Web. 14 January 2011.

CHAPTER 5. PEOPLE: MIXED HERITAGE

1. "Mid-Year Population Estimates 2010." *Statistics South Africa.* Statistics South Africa, 20 July 2010. Web. 22 Jan. 2011.

2. Ibid.

3. Ibid.

4. "The World Factbook: South Africa." *Central Intelligence Agency.* Central Intelligence Agency, 20 Jan. 2011. Web. 26 Jan. 2011.

5. Ibid.

6. "The World Factbook: South Africa." *Central Intelligence Agency.* Central Intelligence Agency, 20 Jan. 2011. Web. 26 Jan. 2011.

7. "South Africa's Population." *SouthAfrica.info.* Brand South Africa, n.d. Web. 15 Feb. 2011.

8. "The World Factbook: South Africa." *Central Intelligence Agency.* Central Intelligence Agency, 20 Jan. 2011. Web. 26 Jan. 2011.

9. "Project Plans; Soweto: Status Quo, Context." *Joburg.org.za.* The Official Web Site of the City of Johannesburg, 2010. Web. 15 Jan. 2011.

10. "South Africa's People." *South African Government Information. Government Communications and Information System [South Africa],* 5 July 2010. Web. 22 Jan. 2011.

SOURCE NOTES CONTINUED

CHAPTER 6. CULTURE: THE RAINBOW NATION
1. "Communications." *South African Government Information*. Government Communications and Information System [South Africa], 5 July 2010. Web. 22 Jan. 2011.

CHAPTER 7. POLITICS: A NEW DEMOCRACY
1. "Elections." *South African Government Information*. Government Communications and Information System [South Africa], 20 July 2010. Web. 14 Jan. 2011.

2. "Constitution of the Republic of South Africa." *South African Government Information*. Government Communications and Information System [South Africa], 21 July 2009. Web. 14 Jan. 2011.

3. "Chapter 2: Bill of Rights." *South African Government Information*. Government Communications and Information System [South Africa], 19 Aug. 2009. Web. 14 Jan. 2011.

4. "The Constitution of South Africa. SouthAfrica.info. BrandSouthAfrica.com, n.d. Web. 22 Jan. 2011.

5. "Preamble." *South African Government Information*. Government Communications and Information System [South Africa], 19 Aug. 2009. Web. 14 Jan. 2011.

6. "Government System." South Africa Yearbook 2009/10. Government Communications [South Africa], 23 Aug. 2010. Web. 26 Jan. 2011.

7. "Chapter 5: The President and National Executive." South African Government Information. Government Communications and Information System [South Africa], 19 August 2009. Web. 14 Jan. 2011.

8. "National and Provincial Elections Results." Independent Electoral Commission South Africa. IEC, 2011. Web. 14 Jan. 2011.

9. "National and Provincial Elections Results." Independent Electoral Commission South Africa. IEC, 2011. Web. 14 Jan. 2011.

10. "National and Provincial Elections Results." *Independent Electoral Commission South Africa*. IEC, 2011. Web. 14 Jan. 2011.

CHAPTER 8. ECONOMICS: THE BOUNTY OF THE LAND
1. "Mining and Minerals in South Africa." *SouthAfrica.info*. BrandSouthAfrica.com, May 2008. Web. 22 Jan. 2011.

2. John Lambert. "Andru Mining: A Welcome Change." *Energy Digital Global Energy Portal*. White Digital Media Group, 10 July 2008. Web. 15 Feb. 2011.

3. "South African Agriculture." *SouthAfrica.info*. BrandSouthAfrica.com, Oct. 2008. Web. 22 Jan. 2011.

4. "Dynamic Growth." *Wines of South Africa*. WOSA SA, 2009. Web. 26 Jan. 2011.

5. "South Africa's Tourism Industry." *SouthAfrica.info*. BrandSouthAfrica.com, Sept. 2008. Web. 22 Jan. 2011.

6. "Energy." South Africa Yearbook 2009/10. Government Communications [South Africa], 23 Aug. 2010. Web. 26 Jan. 2011.

7. "Countries: South Africa." US Energy Information Administration. US Department of Energy, 2009. Web. 15 Feb. 2011.

8. "Community Survey 2007." Statistics South Africa. Statistics South Africa, 2007. Web. 26 Jan. 2011.

9. "South Africa to Build World's Largest Energy Park." *BuaNews Online*. Government Communications and Information System [South Africa], n.d. Web. 15 Feb. 2011.

10. "Communications." South African *Government Information*. Government Communications and Information System [South Africa], 5 July 2010. Web. 15 Feb. 2011.

11. "The World Factbook: South Africa." *Central Intelligence Agency*. Central Intelligence Agency, 20 Jan. 2011. Web. 26 Jan. 2011.

12. "The World Factbook: South Africa." *Central Intelligence Agency*. Central Intelligence Agency, 20 Jan. 2011. Web. 26 Jan. 2011.

13. "Income and Expenditure of Households 2005/2006." *Statistics South Africa*. Statistics South Africa, 4 Mar. 2008. Web. 22 July 2011.

CHAPTER 9. SOUTH AFRICA TODAY

1. "Overview." *UNICEF South Africa*. UNICEF, n.d. Web. 26 Jan. 2011.

2. "Millennium Development Goals: At a Glance." *United Nations*. United Nations, Sept. 2010. Web. 22 Jan. 2011.

3. "International Human Development Indicators: Adult Literacy Rate." *United Nations Development Program*. United Nations Development Program, 2010. Web. 22 Jan. 2011.

4. "Community Survey 2007." *Statistics South Africa*. Statistics South Africa, 2007. Web. 26 Jan. 2011.

5. "SA's Booming Middle Class." *SouthAfrica.info*. BrandSouthAfrica.com, 24 May 2007. Web. 15 Feb. 2011.

6. "HIV and AIDS in South Africa." *AVERT*. AVERT, 2011. Web. 27 Jan. 2011.

7. "The World Factbook: South Africa." *Central Intelligence Agency*. Central Intelligence Agency, 20 Jan. 2011. Web. 26 Jan. 2011.

8. "Community Survey 2007." *Statistics South Africa*. Statistics South Africa, 2007. Web. 26 Jan. 2011.

9. "Human Settlements." *South African Government Information*. Government Communications and Information System [South Africa], 5 July 2010. Web. 22 Jan. 2011.

10. Nelson Mandela. "Closing Address by President Nelson Mandela in the Debate on the State of the Nation Address, 10 Feb. 1999. *South African Government Information*. Government Communications and Information System [South Africa], 10 Feb. 1999. Web. 28 Oct. 2010.

INDEX

INDEX CONTINUED

PHOTO CREDITS